A Quick History

of

VICTOR

Colorado's
"City of Mines"

by

Leland Feitz

Revised Edition
Copyright 1969
by
LELAND FEITZ

Library of Congress Catalog Card Number 70-15100

Published by
LITTLE LONDON PRESS
716 E. Washington St.
Colorado Springs, Colorado

FOREWORD

At the dawn of the twentieth century, the great Cripple Creek-Victor mining district was one of the liveliest, most prosperous places on the face of the earth.

Gold worth over $18,000,000 was mined there in 1900. Then the population of the camp was more than 55,000. Some 8,000 men were employed at 475 mines. The monthly payroll amounted to $900,000.

Because of its unusual name, the city of Cripple Creek got the attention. **But most of the gold came from Victor.**

Victor, in 1893, was a town of flimsy, false-fronted pine buildings. This was the business center.

Drinking water was scarce in early Victor. Thirty buckets full from this wagon sold for a dollar. (Pioneer Museum, Colorado Springs)

EARLY VICTOR

Even though the early Colorado mining towns of Cripple Creek and Victor boomed in the same gold field during the same years, they were not at all alike. Cripple Creek, at the site of the original strike, was the financial, political, and social center of the great gold camp. Victor, on the other hand, was where the miners lived. It was a working man's town and lacked the sophistication of its bigger "sister-city."

Founded in 1893, two years after Cripple Creek, Victor was located right at the foot of Battle Mountain, the camp's richest hill, and near Lawrence, the earliest settlement in that corner of the mining district. The founders, Frank and Harry Woods, named their town after Victor Adams, one of the area's early homesteaders.

Early Victor looked exactly like a mining town should. Its false-fronted pine buildings faced on dirt streets and boardwalks. Housing there was in great demand. Men paid up to a dollar a night to sleep on a pool table or on the floor in the back of a saloon. At meal time, long lines of hungry men formed in front of the town's eating houses. Water sold for five cents a bucket from horse drawn tank wagons. There were only two or three bath tubs in town.

By 1896, however, Victor with a population nearing 8,000 was well on its way to becoming one of Colorado's leading cities. The fast growth was due largely to the efforts of the Woods brothers and the nearness of the city to the great gold mines of Battle Mountain.

The arrival of the Florence and Cripple Creek Railroad in 1894 and the Midland Terminal Railroad the following year also helped Victor to develop. For then, in addition to being the District's mining center, Victor also became its rail center. The coming of a third railroad, The Colorado Springs and Cripple Creek District, some years later added to the importance of Victor as a shipping center.

Great mills to refine the gold ore were also built in the Victor area. They gave employment to many hundreds and made Victor an important milling center, too.

From the earliest days, Victor was called the "City of Mines" and as a mining town, it had few rivals. Even Cripple Creek was jealous of the tremendous output of Victor's gold mines.

This was Victor a few months after its founding in 1893 by Frank and Harry Woods. The Independence, the gold camp's first important mine, is in the foreground. Its discoverer, Winfield Scott Stratton, became the District's first millionaire. (Denver Public Library Western Collection)

Early Victor under a blanket of snow. At an elevation of 9,900 feet heavy snow often falls as early as Labor Day. (State Historical Society of Colorado)

Hotel Victor stood at the corner of Victor Avenue and Fourth Street. It was the city's finest pre-fire hostelry. (Denver Public Library Western Collection)

The lobby of Hotel Victor was a favorite meeting place during the 1890's when fortunes were being made and lost every day in the gold camp. (Denver Public Library Western Collection)

The Fourth of July was the annual celebration the miners looked forward to with the most excitement. Thousands turned out to see the long parades on Victor's streets. (Denver Public Library Western Collection)

Victor, July 4, 1895. The huge holiday crowd is pictured at the corner of Victor Avenue and Fourth Street in front of the old Victor Hotel.

The homes of many of Victor's residents were built high up on Battle Mountain close to the big mines. Rich ore was often turned up as basements for houses were dug. (Denver Public Library Western Collection)

Victor as it looked from Squaw Mountain in 1895. This was the Victor that was soon to be consumed in flames. (Denver Public Library Western Collection)

The Gold Coin, Victor's immense downtown mine. In the foreground, a Florence and Cripple Creek passenger train is seen arriving at the Victor depot. The little narrow gauge provided the gold camp with its first rail service, arriving there from the plains in 1891.

On August 21, 1899, much of Victor was leveled by a fire which started in one of the town's dives. The huge black clouds of smoke were seen as far away as Colorado Springs. (Denver Public Library Western Collection)

VICTOR BURNS

On an August afternoon in 1899, much of Victor was leveled by a fire almost as bad as the ones which had wiped out Cripple Creek three years earlier. Twelve blocks of Victor's business district with some 200 buildings were totally demolished. Losses were estimated at $2,000,000. Over 3,000 were left homeless.

The fire started in a pine shack in Paradise Alley behind the 999 Dance Hall on Portland Avenue between Third and Fourth streets. It leaped from one flimsy pine building to another. A strong wind helped to fan the flames through the downtown section and then up the lower slopes of Battle Mountain. It burned out there late in the evening, three and a half hours after it started.

The next day dawned bright and clear in Victor. At the very first glint of light, hundreds of men went to work clearing away the ruins and building makeshift shacks. By noon, the new Victor post office was completed and people were getting their mail as usual. Even earlier, saloons and restaurants were back in business in tents.

After raging through the business district, the fire destroyed the shaft house and all the impressive surface buildings of the Gold Coin Mine. Minutes after this picture was taken, the posh new Gold Coin Club building (X) was in flames. (State Historical Society of Colorado)

— 11 —

In its path up Battle Mountain the fire destroyed Victor's new depot. (State Historical Society of Colorado)

Thousands of people were left without homes by the Victor fire. Many found temporary refuge on the slopes of Battle Mountain above the charred city. Cripple Creek, destroyed by fire three years earlier, opened her homes and pocketbooks to Victor's homeless. Even though the two towns were bitter rivals, they were always quick to help one another in times of crisis. (State Historical Society of Colorado)

Only a few days after the Victor fire, The Bank of Victor was back in business in this makeshift shack on South Third Street. On the day this picture was taken, $89,688.18 was deposited there and checks worth $163,846.13 were cashed. (Denver Public Library Western Collection. Photo by James Harlan)

VICTOR BUILDS

Almost before the ashes cooled, Victor started to build again. On the second day after the fire, more than 1,000 men were at work on a new Victor. Brick buildings were under construction only five days after the fire.

In only eight months time, a totally new city had been built. This is what **The Denver Republican** reported in April of 1900:

> "Victor has risen to her glory from the piled char heap of late August like a blossoming rose bush. Where before stood cabins, huts and tents, fine brick buildings have shot up like mushrooms during the night."

Victor, then, boasted a population of over 18,000. It was the fifth largest city in Colorado and one of the most modern mining towns on earth. With a monthly payroll amounting to hundreds of thousands of dollars, Victor was also one of the nation's most prosperous places.

Victor, in 1900, was the fifth largest city in the state of Colorado. Its population was 18,000. All new as a result of the fire, it was one of the West's most modern cities. (State Historical Society of Colorado)

The First National was one of Victor's two strong banks. Much of the gold was dug from directly under it.

Streetcars passed down Victor Avenue, the mining town's "main street" every few minutes. This was a street of banks, shops, hotels, and the imposing Victor Grand, the District's largest and finest opera house.

Victor loved a parade! Because it was such a strong union town, the Labor Day parade was the year's longest. As many as fifteen bands marched in the Labor Day parades. (State Historical Society of Colorado)

Ringling Brothers Circus and most all the other big tent shows played the District during the boom. The big top here is being raised at the corner of Victor Avenue and Fourth Street. The crowd has turned out for the colorful circus parade. (State Historical Society of Colorado)

Rodeo at Victor. Horse racing, too, was a favorite gold camp sport. Special trains were run from Victor to Sportsman Park at Gillette for the races. (State Historical Society of Colorado)

THE GOLD COIN CLUB

Victor's Woods brothers were among the very few millionaires who ever returned anything to the District from which their wealth came. Most of the mining wealth poured into Colorado Springs where it built great business blocks, opera houses, and mansions on posh Wood Avenue.

The Woods brothers themselves lived in the Springs and on the street that was named for them. But they did not forget the District and the hundreds of loyal men who worked for them there.

In 1899, the brothers built the Gold Coin Club in Victor for the recreation of their employees. Only a few months after the club was opened, the new building was leveled by the great Victor fire. It was immediately rebuilt. The opening of the new club was marked by one of the District's gayest affairs. Victor was simply agog over the magnificent building which had been patterned after the New York Athletic Club.

The block-long building housed a ballroom, gymnasium, bowling alleys, pool and game room, a 700-volume library, dining rooms and all the other facilities of a well-appointed club. The club even had its own twenty-five piece band.

The Gold Coin Club, the pride and joy of Victor and the Woods brothers for years, was ultimately turned into a hospital. Later, it became a private home. The handsome old building is still standing, but now, like so many of Victor's other imposing buildings, it, too, stands empty.

High Line Electric cars operated between Victor and Cripple Creek every hour from 6:10 a.m. until 2:10 a.m. A second streetcar system, The Low Line, ran cars between the two cities every thirty minutes every day from 6:00 a.m. until midnight.

The narrow gauge Florence and Cripple Creek Railroad once ran fifty-eight trains a day between Cripple Creek and Victor. This is The Limited between the two cities. (Denver Public Library Western Collection)

Goldfield, just outside Victor was the camp's "family" town. Here there was more interest in the home, schools and churches than in gambling halls and saloons. Sitting on a pretty meadow-like spot, it was the District's most attractive residential community. In 1900 its population was 3,500. (Denver Public Library Western Collection)

Independence, another near neighbor of Victor, boasted a population of 2,000 in 1900. (Denver Public Library Western Collection)

BATTLE MOUNTAIN

Between the time the Independence Mine was discovered in 1891 and when the Ajax closed down in 1962, the mines of fabled Battle Mountain produced over $125,000,000 worth of gold. It was one of the richest hills on earth!

THE PORTLAND MINE was the greatest of them all. It, alone, produced about half of Battle Mountain's gold. At an elevation of 10,240 feet, it was the highest mine on the mountain. Its 700-man payroll was the largest. Its massive surface building sprawled over the biggest area.

THE AJAX MINE out-lived all the District's mines. It operated until 1962 and produced well over $20,000,000 worth of gold. Its 3,500-foot shaft was the deepest in the camp.

THE INDEPENDENCE MINE, discovered by Winfield Scott Stratton on July 4, 1891, made him the District's first multimillionaire and established him as one of the all time great mining kings. After taking some $4,000,000 out of his mine, Stratton sold it to a London company for $11,000,000. Ultimately, the Independence produced over $28,000,000 worth of gold, making it the third ranking mine in the District.

The underground workings of the Independence added up to over eighteen miles of tunnels and drifts. Its ore was so pure a miner could carry out a fortune in his pockets.

THE STRONG MINE, too, rated high on the list of great producers. Some $13,000,000 worth of gold was dug from this treasure chest. One of the best equipped of all the mines, it was within easy walking distance of any part of Victor. Its discoverer, Sam Strong, was shot to death in a Cripple Creek saloon.

THE GOLD COIN MINE, while not on Battle Mountain, was a near enough neighbor to the giants there that it deserves to be mentioned. It stood right in Victor's business district. Much of its rich ore was dug from deep under the city.

The Gold Coin was owned by Frank and Harry Woods who founded Victor. Early in the history of their city, the brothers felt there was a need for a first-class hotel. It was while the foundation for the proposed building was being dug that rich ore was discovered. The hotel plans were junked and the great Gold Coin Mine came into being instead.

Stratton's fabulous Independence Mine, discovered on July 4, 1891. After it had made Stratton a very rich man, he sold it to a London company for $11,000,000.

The Gold Coin, Victor's "downtown" gold mine. The handsome brick building even had stained glass windows which prompted one miner to quit. "It's too damn much like working in a church," he said.

Several of the District's richest mines, including the Mary McKinney, the Doctor Jack Pot and the Chicken Hawk were above Squaw Gulch and the little town of Anaconda where Texas Guinan once lived.

The famed Mary McKinney Mine. It produced over $10,000,000 worth of gold. Its rich ore was shipped in locked box cars.

The Bernard Brothers' great Elkton Mine produced gold worth over $16,000,000. But both brothers died practically penniless.

The immense Economic Mill was, by all odds, the District's most imposing landmark. Built in 1899 by the Woods brothers, it was the largest mill of its kind in the world. Ore from the Gold Coin Mine traveled to it on electric cars via a 4000 foot tunnel through Squaw Mountain. (Pioneer Museum, Colorado Springs)

The Wildhorse Mine on Bull Hill above Midway about half way between Victor and Cripple Creek. It was one of the Woods brother's properties. (Clarence Dodson collection)

The Modoc was one of the lesser known mines but nevertheless a very rich one. Not even a trace of it remains today. (Clarence Dodson collection)

The Pharmacist Mine on top Bull Hill was discovered by a druggist who knew nothing about mining. He became one of the gold camp's twenty-seven millionaires.

Deep in the John A. Logan Gold Mine. The mines of the Cripple Creek-Victor District employed over 8,000 men. $500,000 paydays were not uncommon. (Mr. and Mrs. Gene Weinberger Collection)

The Ajax, producer of over $20,000,000 worth of gold was the last of the big mines to shut down. As late as 1939, it worked two shifts of seventy men each. (Denver Public Library Western Collection)

The Isabella Mine stood 10,460 feet above sea level at Bull Cliffs near Victor. (Clarence Dodson Collection)

The Carlton Drainage Tunnel, completed in 1941, lowered the water level in the big mines so they could be worked to greater depths. The bore was over 32,000 feet long and cost $1,000,000. The water it drained off, at the rate of up to 125,000 gallons per minute, went into the Arkansas River and was used to irrigate farms in Eastern Colorado. (Denver Public Library Western Collection)

THE LABOR WARS

Victor's history was twice marred by labor wars; one in 1894 and a second and more serious one in 1903 and 1904. Both struggles resulted from clashes between the mine owners and the Western Federation of Miners.

The first gold camp labor war was triggered by a strike the union called in an effort to correct wage and hour inequalities. Some violence followed before the strike was settled in favor of labor. A $3 wage for an eight-hour day was agreed upon.

The more serious struggle was touched off in 1903 when a strike was called by the Western Federation of Miners. It was ordered to shut off the supply of ore to non union mills in Colorado City. Between 3,500 and 4,000 men were idle and mining operations in the Cripple Creek District were practically paralyzed.

Several of the mines soon reopened with nonunion labor. Violence followed almost immediately. Fifteen men fell to their deaths in an Independence Mine shaft after a cable had been "fixed." An explosion at the Vindicator Mine killed several more. Trains carrying nonunion men to their jobs were wrecked.

Colorado's governor then put the camp under martial law and sent in the National Guard to keep the peace. By mid-September, over 1,000 troops occupied the District.

The occupation lasted about six months and during that time hundreds of union leaders and workers were rounded up and herded into the dreaded "bull pens" which were not a lot unlike concentration camps. Others were ordered out of the District.

With the coming of spring, the troops were withdrawn and the mines were without the protection they had enjoyed during the occupation. Violence erupted again. On the sixth of June, 1904, the depot at Independence was blown up and thirteen scabs were killed and many others were injured. More were killed in riots on the streets of Victor.

The National Guard was sent in a second time on the governor's orders. Again, the camp was under martial law. Once more union people were herded into "bull pens" and this time, hundreds of them were shipped off to Kansas and New Mexico in box cars. They were dumped with orders not to return to the gold camp.

Within days, the war was over. Organized labor had been totally defeated and the camp never completely recovered from the months of violence.

During the long and bloody labor war of 1903 and 1904, the Cripple Creek - Victor mining District was occupied by the Colorado National Guard. This was Camp Goldfield on Battle Mountain, just above Victor. (Denver Public Library Western Collection)

Many of the mines continued to operate with nonunion labor after the 1903 strike was called. They were protected by men of the Colorado National Guard. This was the Shurtloff Mine. (Denver Public Library Western Collection)

The depot at Independence after the June 6, 1904, explosion. The Colorado Springs Telegraph wrote: "The worst heinous and diabolical crime in the history of Colorado was committed this morning at 2:25 o'clock when twenty-five miners on the night shift of the Findlay Mine were waiting at the Independence depot for the Florence & Cripple Creek train to take them to their homes when an infernal machine of hundreds of pounds of powder was exploded under the platform of the depot. The explosion hurled men into space and mangled and tore the bodies of many so they could not be recognized." (Denver Public Library Western Collection)

Violence often erupted on the streets of Victor during the labor wars. The mobs were quieted by the Colorado National Guard. (Denver Public Library Western Collection)

In 1951, the $1,500,000 Carlton Mill opened between Cripple Creek and Victor with a capacity of 1,000 tons of ore per day. It operated until 1962. Owned by the Golden Cycle Corporation of Colorado Springs, it is still considered the world's largest custom gold mill and one of the best equipped. (Photo by Maxine Adams)

When the Carlton Mill operated, it processed up to 1,000 tons of ore daily. Some 600 tons of average value ore had to be handled to produce one gold brick weighing 75 pounds. This was one of the rod mills which helped to grind the ore into a fine dust. (Denver Public Library Western Collection)

PEOPLE OF VICTOR

Among the many well known people who have lived in Victor at one time or another, **Lowell Thomas** is, no doubt, the best known. Though a native of Ohio, Thomas grew up in Victor and graduated from Victor High School. **Bernard Baruch** worked in a few of the mines on Bull Hill. **Texas Guinan** of New York speakeasy fame grew up in Anaconda Gulch between Victor and Cripple Creek. **Groucho Marx** spent some time working for a District grocer after the show he was traveling with folded in Victor. **Jack Dempsey** once worked at the Portland Mine. **Robert Coates**, art critic for The New Yorker, spent his early years in Victor. **Mr. Gallagher** and **Mr. Shean**, who made it big in the Ziegfield Follies and on the national vaudeville stage, were motormen on the District's trolley system. **Mabel Barbee Lee**, whose "Cripple Creek Days" and "Back in Cripple Creek" were best sellers, taught school in Victor. **Winfield Scott Stratton**, whose Independence Mine made him the gold camp's first multimillionaire, left his fortune to establish the unique Myron Stratton Home for the homeless and aged in Colorado Springs.

The homes of Victor pile up on many levels. The arrow points to the Lowell Thomas boyhood home, now one of the city's two museums. Thomas's father was one of Victor's seventeen doctors. (Photo by Roger Appleton)

Victor today. The population of the "City of Mines" has slipped to about 300. Now "For Sale" and "No Trespassing" signs hang on many of the old buildings which are slowly rotting away.

VICTOR TODAY

Since the end of gold mining in 1962, hard times have indeed come upon the "City of Mines." The town's population has slipped and its economy has been almost totally based on Social Security and pension checks. Victor's streets have been quiet; very quiet.

With the coming of each summer, the old town has shown a little new life. Quite a few of its houses have been purchased by "flatlanders" for summer homes and there has been a fair amount of tourist traffic.

Until Victor booms once again as a gold mining town, and there is every evidence it soon will, the town seems to have a fairly promising future as a tourist attraction.

As in the old days, Victor still lives somewhat in the shadow of its better known neighbor, Cripple Creek. But, those who do bother to discover Victor find it to be one of the country's most picturesque and best preserved mining towns.

Once a city of churches, Victor has only two that are now in use. This is the First Baptist. St. Victor's Catholic Church opens for masses only on the first and third Sundays of every month.

South Fourth was once one of downtown Victor's busy streets. The building with the impressive facade is the Masonic Temple. The little building to its right housed the Victor Record where Lowell Thomas once worked.

The Last Dollar Mine. It was one of the giants, producing over $7,500,000 worth of gold. (Photo by Clarence Dodson)

Stratton's Independence Mine now.

The ruins of the giant Independence Mine mill cover several acres at the edge of Victor. (Photo by Roger Appleton)

The Morning Glory Mine today. It is above Anaconda on the highway between Cripple Creek and Victor. (Photo by Clarence Dodson)

This is all that remains of the Elkton's hoist. It pulled over $16,000,000 worth of gold up from this deep mine.

These are the surface buildings of the famed El Paso Mine. It is open for tours.

The Victor High School building stands at the foot of Battle Mountain under the Ajax. It was the last of the major gold mines to discontinue operating. (Photo by Roger Appleton)

Victor's handsome old Christian Science Church has stood empty for well over three decades. (Photo by Roger Appleton)

The signs on this old Victor Avenue building have weathered there for over half a century.
(Photo by Roger Appleton)

Victor's depot. As many as fifty-eight passenger trains once arrived at this station every day.
(Photo by Roger Appleton)

The "City of Mines" was also a city of fine Victorian homes. Many of them have now become retirement and summer houses. The town has a delightful year around climate and provides all the services expected of a little city.

This old building on South Third Street once housed the popular Little Pittsburgh Saloon. It was one of thirty-seven operating in Victor at the turn of the century.

Houses on South Sixth Street. Half a century ago it was one of Victor's pretty neighborhoods.

An alley in downtown Victor. The old buildings have stood there for over three-quarters of a century. (Photo by Roger Appleton)

Victor's alleys are full of surprises from out of the past. (Photo by Roger Appleton)

There's not much left of once booming Anaconda. (Photo by Roger Appleton)

Many of Victor's pioneers rest in Sunnyside Cemetery about a mile from the little town.

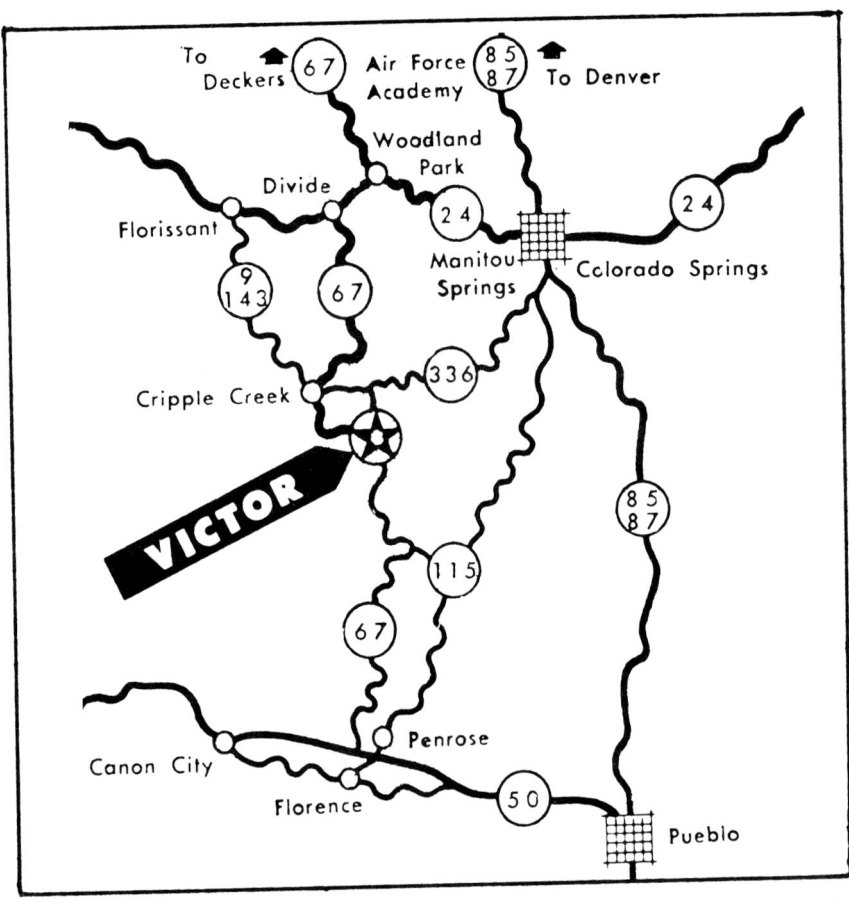

As a mining town, Victor's future looks pretty grim unless, of course, the price of gold were to be increased. Then, Victor might well boom again.

There is still plenty of gold ore in the District's mines, but, at today's price ($35.00 an ounce) and today's high production costs, it simply cannot be mined profitably.

BIBLIOGRAPHY:
BOOKS:

Bowman, George. *The Fabulous Cripple Creek District.* 1958.
Brown, Robert L. *Ghost Towns of the Colorado Rockies.* Caxton, 1968.
Eberhart, Perry. *Guide to Colorado Ghost Towns and Mining Camps.* Sage Books, 1959.
Lee, Mabel Barbee. *Cripple Creek Days.* Doubleday and Company, Inc., 1958.
Mazzulla, Fred and Jo. *First 100 Years.* 1956.
Sprague, Marshall. *Money Mountain.* Little, Brown and Co., 1953
Taylor, Robert Guilford. *Cripple Creek.* Indiana University Publications, 1966.
Waters, Frank. *Midas of the Rockies.* Sage Books, 1949.
Wolle, Muriel Sibell. *Stampede to Timberline.* Sage Books, 1949
Works Progress Administration. *Colorado.* Hastings House. 1941.

PAMPHLETS AND DIRECTORIES:

Cripple Creek District Directory. 1900.
Cripple Creek Mining District. 1897.
Gold Fields of Cripple Creek. 1900.
The World's Famous Gold Camp.
Decade of Millionaires.

NEWSPAPERS:

The Colorado Springs Evening Telegraph.
The Denver Republican.
The Cripple Creek Gold Rush.
The Colorado Springs Gazette Telegraph.
The Denver Post.

By the Same Author
CRIPPLE CREEK!
A Quick History of the World's Greatest Gold Camp
MYERS AVENUE
A Quick History of Cripple Creek's Red Light District
CRIPPLE CREEK RAILROADS
A Quick History of the Great Gold Camp's Railroads
PLATORO
Mining Camp and Resort Town
CREEDE
Colorado Boom Town